Science
made easy

Key Stage 2
Ages 9–10

Authors Mike Evans, Linda Ellis,
Hugh Westrup and David Evans
Consultants David Evans and Kara Pranikoff

Certificate

Congratulations to ....
(write your name here)
for successfully finishing this book.

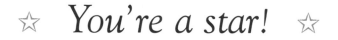 *You're a star!*

What is the life cycle of a butterfly?

Science facts

A butterfly is an insect that looks very different at each stage of its life.
The amazing change in body shape is called metamorphosis.

Science quiz

Use the words in the box to label each stage in the life of a butterfly
and complete the sentences below.

Adult	Caterpillar	Chrysalis	Egg

....

....

1 The .... is a tiny round or oval object. It is often attached
   to a leaf or a stem of a plant.

2 The .... is long and wormlike. It eats and eats to
   grow quickly.

3 The .... is a case that protects the caterpillar as it
   rests while its body changes.

4 The .... emerges with colourful wings and flies away.

What is the life cycle of a grasshopper?

Science facts

A grasshopper is an example of an insect that has the same body shape throughout most of its life.

Science quiz

Use the words to label each stage in the life of a grasshopper and complete the sentences below.

Adult	Nymph	Egg

....

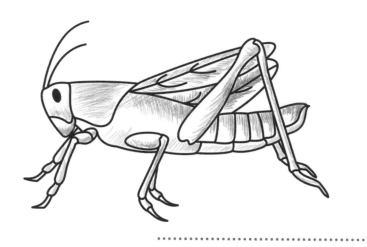

....

1 A grasshopper starts as a tiny ...., usually attached to a leaf or stem.

2 A baby grasshopper is called a ....

3 A fully grown .... grasshopper has large legs for hopping.

What is the life cycle of a frog?

Science facts

A frog is an amphibian, which is a type of animal that spends part of its life in water and part on land. Frogs are very different at each stage of their life cycle. The change in body shape from tadpole to adult is called metamorphosis.

Science quiz

Use the words to label the stages in the life of a frog.

Egg	Frog	Froglet	Tadpole	Tadpole with legs

Why do plants have flowers?

Science facts

Flowers contain the male and female sexual organs of a plant. The petals are brightly coloured and scented to attract insects and other pollinators. The stamen (containing the anther and filament) is the male part. It produces pollen. The carpel, containing the ovary, style and stigma, is the female part. Seeds form when the male cell meets the female cell in the ovary.

Science quiz

Write the correct numbers in the circles below to show the name of each part of the flower. You may need to look in a reference book for help.

1 Ovary	2 Style	3 Anther	4 Filament	5 Petal	6 Sepal	7 Stigma

Science activity

Not all flowers have the same structure as the one shown above, but you can find all these parts in most flowers. Gather some flowers from a garden or buy some from a shop. Take them apart carefully. Display the parts of each flower by sticking the bits on a piece of white card. Label the parts.

How are flowers pollinated?

Science facts

The process by which pollen gets transferred from one flower to another is called pollination. This transfer can happen in different ways. Insects such as bees are attracted to bright, scented flowers. They go into the flower to gather nectar and the spiky pollen sticks to their bodies. The sticky stigmas on other flowers catch the pollen when the insect brushes past them. Some flowers use the wind to carry pollen. Their dangling stamens produce lots of light pollen that is blown about by the wind.

The stigmas of these plants are feathery and hang outside the flower to catch the pollen as it floats by.

Science quiz

The parts of some flowers are described below. Write **Insect** if you think they belong to insect-pollinated flowers or **Wind** for wind-pollinated flowers.

1 The stigmas are sticky.   ....

2 The stamens are dangling out of the flower.   ....

3 The petals are bright red and smell nice.   ....

4 The stamens are inside the flower.   ....

5 The stigmas are feathery.   ....

6 The petals are small and green.   ....

7 The flower is very small.   ....

Science activity

(!) You may be surprised to know that grass has flowers. They are not very pretty or scented as they are pollinated by the wind and do not have to attract insects.
In summer, try and find some grass flowers.
Use a magnifying glass to look for
the feathery stigmas and stamens.

How do seeds germinate in the wild?

Science facts

Seeds need air, moisture and warmth to germinate, or sprout. They do not need soil. Some kinds of seed need to be frozen before they can germinate and a few rare species can only germinate after forest fires. Most seeds will germinate in either a light or a dark place, but some germinate faster in the dark and others in the light.

Science quiz

Explain how you could set up a fair test to show that a broad-bean seed does not need to be in the dark to germinate. Describe how you would use broad-bean seeds, cotton wool, water and two containers to set up your test.

....

....

....

....

Science activity

Do seeds from different plants take different amounts of time to germinate? Set up an experiment to find out. You can try germinating a variety of seeds on damp cotton wool.

How quickly do we grow?

Science facts

Most animals have similar patterns of growth. In general, they grow when they are young and stop at adulthood. Girls and boys grow at different rates. Rates of growth and size at maturity are also affected by such things as diet and heredity. For example, tall parents are likely to have offspring who grow into tall adults.

Science quiz

These charts show the heights of some girls and boys. They were measured in Year 1, then again in Year 3 and in Year 5. Find out how much each child has grown by working out the difference between their heights in the four years between Year 1 and Year 5. Fill in each growth box.

Girls	Height in cm			
Name	Year 1	Year 3	Year 5	Growth
Susan	110	116	128	
Dela	109	116	130	
Farida	102	110	121	
Jasmine	112	118	126	

Boys	Height in cm			
Name	Year 1	Year 3	Year 5	Growth
Jack	110	115	126	
Liang	112	119	126	
Dave	112	120	131	
Naresh	100	105	111	

Which child grew the most in four years? ....

What was the average growth of the girls? ....

What was the average growth of the boys? ....

Did all the girls grow at the same rate? ....

Did all the boys grow at the same rate? ....

Did the girls or the boys grow faster? ....

Science activity

⚠ Soak a broad-bean seed in water overnight. Plant the seed in some potting compost. Cover it with a plastic bag and leave it in a warm place, watering it regularly. After a few days, a shoot should grow. Record the shoot's height each day for two weeks. Draw a graph of the shoot's growth.

How long is a life cycle?

Science facts

Animals and plants have life cycles. There is a period of development before they are born. This is called the gestation period. Then, there is a period of growth that leads to maturity, when they can reproduce. The offspring then begin their own life cycles. In humans, the gestation period and the time taken to reach maturity are very long. The growth phase is divided into several stages: babyhood, childhood and adolescence.

Science quiz

Study this chart carefully and answer the questions that follow.

Animal	Gestation period (days)	Age at maturity
Human	270 days	14 years
Bear	230 days	4 years
Horse	336 days	2 years
Dog	63 days	15 months
Cat	60 days	9 months
Elephant	624 days	14 years
Mouse	20 days	6 weeks

Which animal has the longest gestation period?..

Which animal reaches maturity in the shortest time?......................................

Is there a link between the age at maturity and the size of the animal?

....

....

Science activity

Ask an adult you know well if you can have some photos of him or her as a baby, a child, an adolescent and a parent. Put the photos in order of age. Draw a time line on a big piece of paper. Mark each year on it and stick the photos beside the right years. Label each stage of development.

Which metal is this?

Science facts

A metal is a type of material. Almost all metals are shiny, malleable (can be hammered into different shapes) and conduct heat and electricity. There are different types of metal, such as iron, copper, gold, lead and tin. Each metal has a set of additional properties that makes it unique.

Science quiz

Use the branching Yes/No key below to identify each of the five metals in this chart. Write the correct letter for each metal below its name.

	Properties
A	Hard; brown in colour; good conductor of electricity
B	Relatively soft; yellow colour; does not tarnish; very good conductor of electricity
C	Soft; silver colour; tarnishes quickly; very heavy; a weak conductor of electricity
D	Hard; silver colour; magnetic; tarnishes easily (rusts)
E	Hard; silver colour; does not tarnish easily; not magnetic

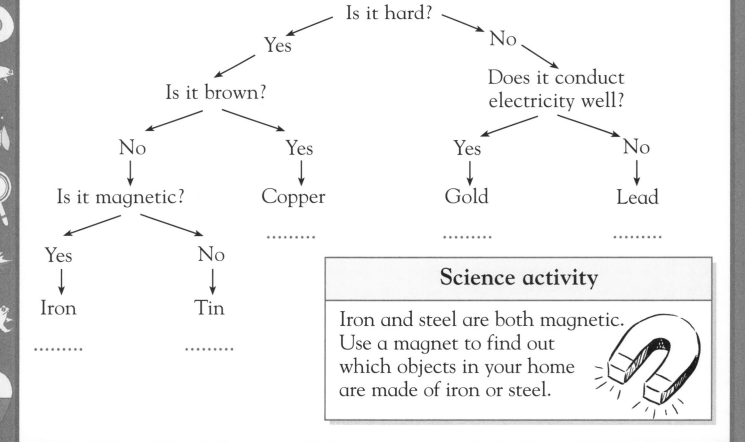

Is it hard?

Yes → Is it brown?

No → Is it magnetic?

Yes → Iron ....

No → Tin ....

Yes → Copper ....

No → Does it conduct electricity well?

Yes → Gold ....

No → Lead ....

Science activity

Iron and steel are both magnetic. Use a magnet to find out which objects in your home are made of iron or steel.

Is it an electrical conductor?

Science facts

A material that allows electricity to pass through it easily is called an electrical conductor. Many metals are good electrical conductors.

Science quiz

An electrical circuit was set up to test whether or not some materials are conductors. If the material conducts electricity, the bulb in the circuit lights up. The better the conductor, the brighter the bulb. Here are the results.

Material tested	Status of lamp
Gold	Very bright
Copper	Bright
Plastic	Not lit
Wood	Not lit
Graphite	Quite bright
Lead	Quite bright
Paper	Not lit
Sea water	Bright
Pure water	Not lit

Most metals conduct electricity. Can you identify the metals in the chart?

....

Which one is the best conductor? ....

Which solid non-metal conducts electricity? Where do you usually find this?

....

Why do you think sea water conducts electricity but pure water does not?

....

Science activity

(!) Make a circuit using a battery, wires and a bulb. Use your circuit to find some more materials that conduct electricity.

Is it a thermal insulator?

Science facts

Materials that allow heat to pass through them easily are called thermal conductors. Metals and glass are good thermal conductors. Some materials do not conduct heat well. They are called thermal insulators. Materials such as plastics, wood, wool and air are good thermal insulators.

Science quiz

Five glasses containing water at 60°C were each wrapped in a different material. After 10 minutes, the water temperature in each glass was recorded. The results are shown in the table below.

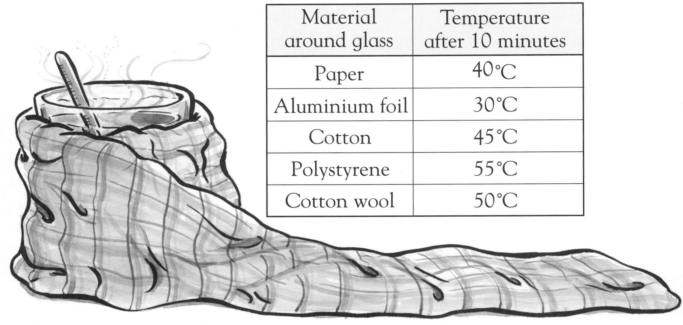

Material around glass	Temperature after 10 minutes
Paper	40°C
Aluminium foil	30°C
Cotton	45°C
Polystyrene	55°C
Cotton wool	50°C

Which material would you choose to wrap around a water pipe in winter to stop the water from freezing? Explain why.

....

....

....

Science activity

Fill two yogurt pots with water. Record the temperature in each pot and then put on the lids. Cover one pot in a thick layer of lard. Put them both in a freezer for 20 minutes and then record the water temperature again. What do your results tell you about why whales and seals living in cold waters have thick layers of body fat?

How soluble are materials?

Science facts

Substances that can be dissolved in a liquid are said to be soluble. Those that do not dissolve are said to be insoluble. The liquid in which a substance dissolves is called a solvent. The substance that is dissolved is called a solute. Together, they make a solution. Water is a good solvent: it dissolves many substances but not all. Sugar and salt both dissolve in water, while substances such as chalk and sand are insoluble.

Science quiz

Shakira collected two different plant fertilisers from a garden centre. She was told to mix each fertiliser with water and then to sprinkle the solution on her plants. When she mixed them, the first substance "disappeared". The fertiliser in the second can sank to the bottom.

The fertiliser in the second watering can would not be very effective. Why?

....

....

Science activity

Collect some substances such as flour, Epsom salts, icing sugar, sand, baking powder, bicarbonate of soda and cooking oil. Design a way of finding out which substances are soluble in water and which are insoluble.

Are all substances equally soluble?

Science facts

All soluble substances do not dissolve equally well. Sugar dissolves very easily, while other substances, such as salt, dissolve less easily. The amount of solute that will dissolve in a solvent is a measure of its solubility.

Science quiz

Below is a graph showing the solubility of different substances.

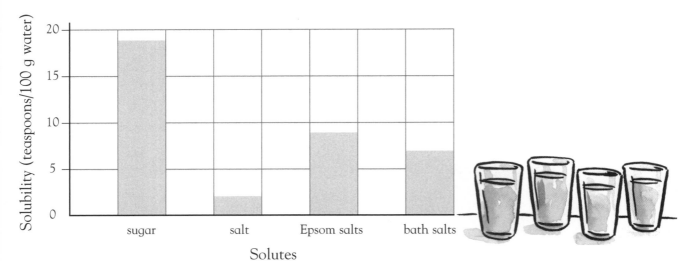

About how many spoonfuls of salt dissolve in the water? ....

About how many spoonfuls of bath salts dissolve in the water? ....

Another substance is more soluble than bath salts but less soluble than Epsom salts. What range of spoonfuls would you expect to dissolve? ....

List the solutes in the chart in order of their solubility.
Write the name of the most soluble substance first.

....

Science activity

Does the grain size of sugar affect its solubility? Design and carry out an experiment to answer this question.

Can you separate salt from sand?

Science facts

Filtering removes insoluble particles from water (particles that do not dissolve). Salt is soluble in water, but sand is not soluble (it is insoluble). The water in a salt solution will evaporate if it is left uncovered. Rock salt is a mixture of salt and sand.

Science quiz

Using the information above, explain how you could separate the salt from a piece of rock salt. Drawing a flowchart might help.

Science activity

What type of paper makes the best filter? Design an experiment to find out. You will need a funnel and different kinds of paper, including newspaper, writing paper, blotting paper, wrapping paper and tissue paper.

Can we filter things?

Science facts

If the materials in a mixture are insoluble, you can use a filter to separate them. A filter has holes in it. Coffee grounds are insoluble in water. When you pour a mixture of coffee grounds and water into a filter, the holes in the filter are large enough for the liquid to drain away, but too small for the grounds to pass through. The coffee grounds are trapped by the filter.

Science quiz

Here are some lentils, peas and marbles all mixed up in a pot. Pictures A and B show the bottom of the pot. On A, draw the sizes of holes you must make to separate the lentils from the peas and marbles. On B, draw the holes you would need to make to separate the lentils and peas from the marbles.

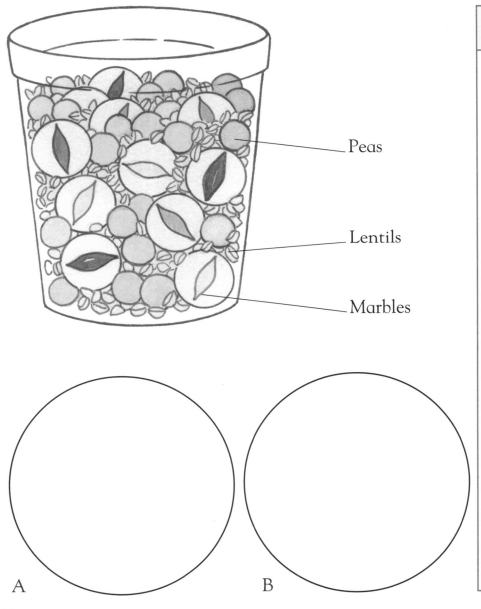

Peas

Lentils

Marbles

A   B

Science activity

(!) Try filtering out the different sized particles of soil. You can use a flowerpot with holes in it to remove larger stones. Then squeeze the remains through an old pair of tights. Only the tiniest soil particles will get through. (Always wear gloves when you handle soil.)

How can we separate mixtures?

Science facts

Mixtures of materials can be separated in different ways. To find out which is the best way to separate a mixture, you must first ask yourself some important questions. For example, are any of the materials in the mixture soluble? Are any of the materials attracted to a magnet? Do any of the materials change when they are heated? What size are the particles in the materials?

Science quiz

On the left, you can see four different mixtures. On the right are four different methods of separating mixtures. Draw a line between each mixture and the correct separation method.

Steel nails and copper nails

Dissolve in water and then use a filter.

Rice and mung beans

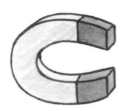

Use a magnet.

Soil containing mud and sand

Use a colander.

Sand and salt

Shake in a bottle with some water and leave to settle.

Which fabric will stretch the most?

Science facts

Materials that stretch easily are called elastic materials. Some materials are more elastic than others. We can compare the elasticity of two materials by hanging equal weights from them and measuring how much they stretch.

Science quiz

Poppy tried to compare the stretch in five different fabrics. All the fabrics were the same length to begin with. Her table of results is shown below.

Fabric	Weight hung from fabric	Amount of stretch
Cotton	10 N	3 cm
Wool	100 N	40 cm
Nylon	100 N	55 cm
Polyester	500 N	200 cm
Tercel	10 N	3 cm

Which material stretched the most?

....

How could Poppy have improved her experiment?

....

....

Science activity

Design an experiment to find out which brand of tights stretches the most.

Which is the strongest wood?

Science facts

Strength is an important property of materials. It is a measure of a material's resistance to breaking. You can compare the strengths of different materials by hanging increasingly heavier weights from them until they break.

Science quiz

Lata hung weights on strips of wood until the wood broke in the middle.

Type of wood	Weight needed to break wood (in newtons)
Beech	2000 N
Oak	3000 N
Walnut	2600 N
Ash	2500 N
Pine	500 N
Sycamore	2500 N

Use the data in the table above to work out which type of wood you would choose to build a bridge. Explain your choice.

....

....

Science activity

⚠ Collect some twigs of the same width from different types of tree. Hang a bag from each twig and then suspend the twigs between two table tops. Load each bag with the same weight (such as a can of beans) until the twigs break. Which is the strongest twig?

Are some changes reversible?

Science facts

When ice is warmed, it melts to form water. When water is heated further, it evaporates or boils to form water vapour. These changes from solid to liquid to gas can be reversed by cooling water vapour. The water vapour will condense to form water, and the water will freeze to form ice.

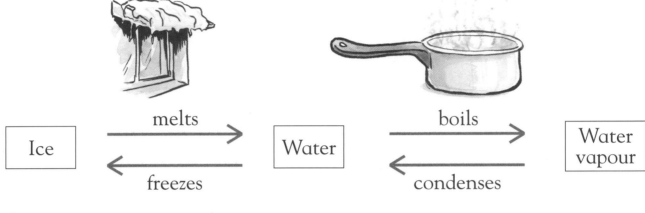

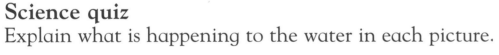

Ice → melts → Water → boils → Water vapour
← freezes ← ← condenses ←

Science quiz

Explain what is happening to the water in each picture.

....

....

....

....

....

....

Science activity

Light a candle and watch it carefully (do not touch it or get too close). Can you identify the solid wax, melted wax and wax vapour? Can you see the liquid wax solidifying when the flame is put out?

Are some changes irreversible?

Science facts

When you mix substances together, they may change to form new substances.
The changes can be reversible or irreversible. For instance, when vinegar is
mixed with bicarbonate of soda, the two fizz and a new substance is formed.
This change is irreversible. A change is likely to be irreversible if there is
a reaction, such as a fizz or a temperature change.

Science quiz

Are the following mixing processes reversible or irreversible?

1 Stirring sugar into water   ....

2 Adding water to plaster of Paris   ....

3 Mixing sand and sugar   ....

4 Adding lemon juice to red-cabbage juice
   (the colour changes from purple to red)   ....

Science activity

Try mixing the following substances.
Which changes are reversible?
1 Lemon juice added to baking powder
2 Vinegar added to chalk
3 Vinegar added to salt
4 Lemon juice added to sugar

Where is each planet?

Science facts

There are eight planets in the solar system. In order from the Sun, they are: Mercury, Venus, Earth, Mars, Jupiter, Saturn, Uranus and Neptune.

Science quiz

The planets are shown here in their order from the Sun. Label each one correctly. They are not shown to scale.

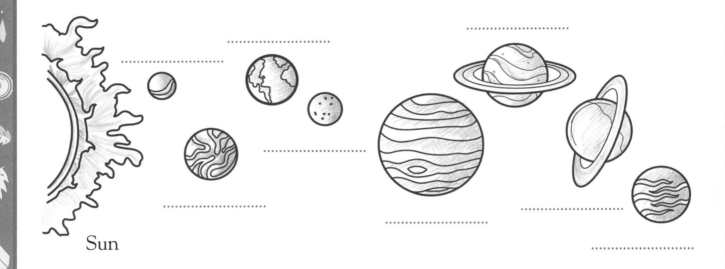

Sun

Answer these questions about the planets.

Which is the biggest planet? ....

Which planet is nearest to the Sun? ....

Which planet is farthest from the Sun? ....

Which planet is closest to Earth? ....

Which planets are surrounded by rings? ....

Although this planet lies second from the Sun,
it is the hottest of them all. ....

Which planet looks tilted on its side, because
its rings orbit from top to bottom? ....

Does the Moon change shape?

Science facts

The Moon is not a light source. Light from the Sun is reflected off the surface of the Moon, allowing us to see it. The Moon makes a complete orbit around the Earth in about 28 days. You can see either a whole, round Moon reflecting light or just a part of it depending on where it is in its orbit.

The Moon's changing appearance during one month as seen from Earth.

New Moon   Earth   Full Moon

Science quiz

The chart below shows how the Moon appears from the Earth during various dates in January. Can you work out the missing shapes?

Date in January	Moon's appearance
1st	
6th	
10th	
15th	
19th	
24th	
28th	

Science activity

You can model the way the Moon appears as it orbits the Earth. Use a torch to represent the Sun and a table-tennis ball for the Moon. Ask a friend to hold the torch still in a darkened room. Hold the ball at arm's length in front of the torch. Turn around slowly in a circle, keeping your eyes fixed on the ball. Can you see the reflection of the light on the ball? Does it look like the different phases of the Moon?

What shape is the Earth?

Science facts

Stars and planets are spherical. Stars are balls of burning gas that produce heat and light. Planets are made of rock, gas and sometimes frozen liquid. Some have spherical moons that travel around them. Our Solar System contains a star, called the Sun, and eight planets.

Science quiz

Imagine you are travelling in a spacecraft and are able to look out of the window at our part of the Solar System. Which of these pictures would you be most likely to see? Tick (✔) the right box.

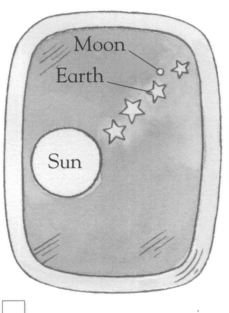

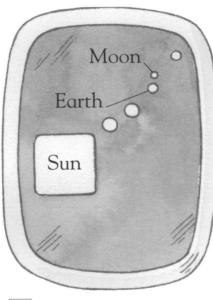

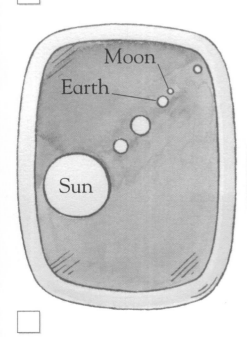

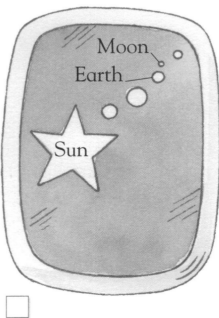

Science activity

Find out the names of the eight planets in the Solar System. What is each planet made of? Which is the biggest planet and which is the smallest? Which of the planets have moons? Use books or the Internet to find out the answers.

Why does the Sun appear to move?

Science facts

The Sun appears to move across the sky during the course of the day. In fact, it is the Earth that moves and not the Sun. The Earth makes one complete turn around its axis every 24 hours, or once a day. The Sun appears to rise in the east, when the part of the Earth you are on is turning towards the Sun, and appears to set in the west, when your hometown is turning away from the Sun. As well as spinning on its axis, the Earth orbits around the Sun. It takes the Earth 365 days, or one year, to make one complete orbit around the Sun.

Science quiz

The picture shows the Sun at three times during one day. First it was in position A, then B and finally C.

Which side of the picture is the east? ....

What time is it at position B? ....

About what time is it at position C? ....

Science activity

On a sunny morning, stand a 50-cm-long stick in the ground in your garden or local park. Mark the position of the end of the stick's shadow with a piece of chalk. Repeat this every hour so that by evening you have at least seven marks on the ground. What pattern can you see? Explain why the shadow moved.

What causes night and day?

Science facts

The Earth completes one turn around its axis every 24 hours. When the part of the Earth where you live faces the Sun, it is daytime. Sunrise, also called dawn, occurs when the part of the Earth where you are turns enough for you to just see the Sun. At sunset, just before night, the Earth has turned so that again you can only just see the Sun. When it is night where you are, it is daytime for people living on the other side of the Earth.

Science quiz

One evening, David, who lives in London, England, was allowed to phone his uncle who lives in Montreal, Canada. David was very surprised to hear that his uncle was just about to have his midday meal.

What is the explanation for this difference in time?

....

....

....

Science activity

Make a model of the Sun and the Earth. Use a torch to represent the Sun and a football to represent the Earth. Do this experiment in a darkened room. Put your torch on a table so that it shines into the room. Hold the football about 1 metre away from the torch and turn it around slowly. The football is like the Earth turning on its axis. Draw a mark on your ball with a pencil. Spin your ball slowly. Notice how the light only falls on the mark for about half of the spin. This is like daytime. When the light does not shine on the mark, it is like night.

What makes things fall?

Science facts

Gravity is a type of force. It is a pull, or force of attraction, between two objects. The bigger the object, the bigger the attraction. The Earth is a huge object and everything on the Earth is pulled towards the Earth's centre. We call the pull between us and the Earth our weight. Force is measured in units called newtons. The pull of gravity on us, our weight, can be measured in newtons. The force on each kilogram is about 10 newtons. This means that the heavier you are, the more force gravity has on you.

Science quiz

Draw an arrow to show the direction of the force extending the spring.

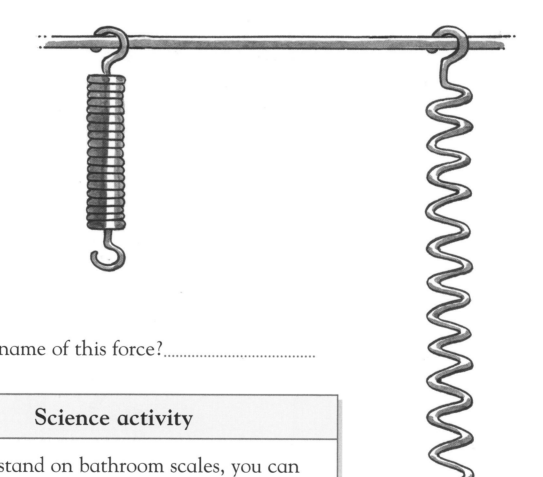

What is the name of this force?...................................

Science activity

When you stand on bathroom scales, you can find out how heavy you are in kilograms (kg). Use your bathroom scales to work out how much force you exert on the Earth due to gravity pulling you down. Remember, the force on 1 kilogram is 10 newtons.

Does a force have a direction?

Science facts

A force is a push or a pull. Forces can move things or stop them from moving. They can make things speed up or slow down. Forces can also make things change direction. For example, the force of the wind can blow a boat off course. A force acts in one direction. This direction is shown in diagrams by using arrows. A longer arrow is used to show a bigger force.

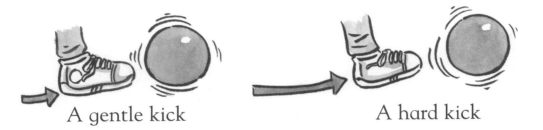

A gentle kick   A hard kick

Science quiz

Look at the diagrams below. On each diagram, draw an arrow to show the direction of each force mentioned.

The pull of gravity on the spring

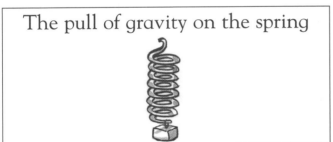

The force of friction slowing the rolling can

The force of the hammer

The force exerted by each team (2 arrows)

Science activity

Use a newtonmeter to measure some forces. Compare the forces needed to open a door, to drag a pencil case or to lift a cup. Then, draw each object and use an arrow to show the direction in which the newtonmeter is pulled.

How do parachutes work?

Science facts

Gravity is a pulling force. It pulls objects towards the Earth. Air resistance is a pushing force. Parachutes use air resistance to slow down falling objects. The air caught under the parachute pushes against the fabric's surface, slowing it down. The bigger the parachute, the more slowly it will fall. This is because more air pushes against larger surfaces and so there is more air resistance.

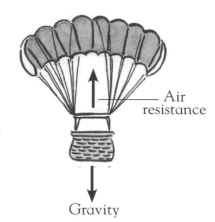

Air resistance

Gravity

Science quiz

Look at this drawing of two people jumping with parachutes.

Which one will fall to Earth faster? Explain your answer.

....

....

What is the name of the force pulling the people and their parachutes down?

....

Science activity

Find out if your answers in the quiz are correct. Make two parachutes using handkerchiefs or paper towels, cotton thread and two identical small weights, such as nuts. Make one parachute larger than the other. Drop them from the same height. Which one falls faster?

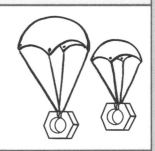

What makes boats float?

Science facts

An object floats or sinks depending on a combination of the object's shape and weight. When an object is placed in water, the water pushes the object upwards – this force is called the upthrust. If enough water pushes it up, the upthrust will be greater than gravity and the object will float.

Upthrust   Gravity

Science quiz

Objects weigh less in water than in air because of the upthrust of water. David used a newtonmeter to measure and compare the weights of different objects in air and in water. His results are given in the table below.

Object	Weight in air (N)	Weight in water (N)
Stone	130 N	6 N
Wood block	20 N	0 N
Plastic hair clip	5 N	1 N
Metal pan	500 N	0 N

Use the table above to work out which objects will float. Explain how you came to your conclusions.

....

....

Science activity

Take a lump of modelling clay. Place it in a bowl of water. Does it float or sink? Can you find a way to shape the clay so that it will float? How many shapes can you make that will float? Can you explain why these shapes float?

What effect does friction have?

Science facts

Friction is a force that slows things down. Whenever two surfaces come into contact, there is a frictional force. The amount of frictional force (how much it slows things down) depends on the roughness of the surfaces and on the force pressing them together. For example, if two plastic balls of the same size but different weights are given a push of the same strength, the lighter ball will go farther because there is less friction slowing it down.

Science quiz

Amber covered a plank with different materials and measured how far a wooden block slid on each surface before coming to a halt. Here are her results.

Type of surface	How far the block slid after being pushed
Sandpaper	50 cm
Glass	500 cm
Wood	100 cm
Plastic	300 cm
Cardboard	190 cm

Which is the smoothest surface and which is the roughest surface?

....

Explain how you worked out the answers to the question above.

....

....

Science activity

Use a plank of wood, a toy block, sticky tape, and different materials, such as paper, polythene and sandpaper, to compare the roughness of their surfaces. Tape one material to the plank. Place the block on it and lift one end of the plank until the block slides down. Repeat with the other materials. Which material provides the most friction?

How does a lever work?

Science facts
The point at which a lever turns is called a fulcrum. The fulcrum needs to be in the right place for the lever to work properly.

Science quiz
Using the objects pictured below, carry out the instructions.

30-cm ruler

Pencil with flat sides

Several dozen coins

1 Set up the test as shown above. The ruler is the lever.
2 Slide the pencil under the ruler at the 10-cm mark. This is the lever's fulcrum, or pivot.
3 Stack 5 coins between the end of the ruler and the 2.5-cm mark.
4 At the other end of the ruler, stack coins one at a time until the end with the 5 coins rises off the table.
5 Place the pencil at different positions under the ruler, as shown in the table on the right, and repeat the test.
6 Record the number of coins it takes to lift the 5 coins with the fulcrum at each of the different positions.

Position of pencil under ruler	Number of coins
7.5 cm	
10 cm	
12.5 cm	
15 cm	

Answer Section with Parents' Notes
Key Stage 2
Ages 9–10

This section provides answers and explanatory notes to the quizzes and activities in the book. Work through each page together and ensure that your child understands each task. Point out any mistakes in your child's work and correct any errors, but also remember to praise your child's efforts and achievements. Where appropriate, ask your child to predict the outcome of the *Science activity* experiments. After each experiment, challenge your child to explain the results.

(!) If a *Science activity* box includes this caution symbol, extra care is necessary. In such cases, experiments may involve heavy weights, sharp objects, hot water, ice or soil. Always wear gloves when handling soil and ensure hands are washed afterwards. Gloves are also advisable for activities in which hot or very cold objects are used.

---

2 ☆ ## What is the life cycle of a butterfly?

Science facts
A butterfly is an insect that looks very different at each stage of its life. The amazing change in body shape is called metamorphosis.

Science quiz
Use the words in the box to label each stage in the life of a butterfly and complete the sentences below.

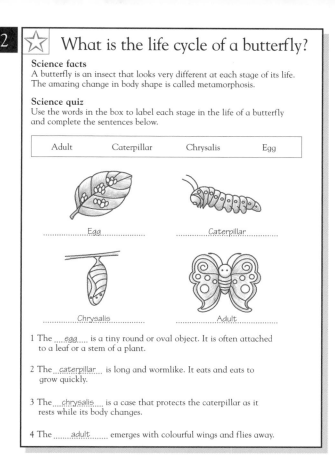

| Adult | Caterpillar | Chrysalis | Egg |

Egg   Caterpillar

Chrysalis   Adult

1 The __egg__ is a tiny round or oval object. It is often attached to a leaf or a stem of a plant.

2 The __caterpillar__ is long and wormlike. It eats and eats to grow quickly.

3 The __chrysalis__ is a case that protects the caterpillar as it rests while its body changes.

4 The __adult__ emerges with colourful wings and flies away.

Explain the difference between a chrysalis and a cocoon to your child. A cocoon is a protective coat of silk spun by some types of moth for their metamorphosis. It is different from a butterfly's chrysalis. Butterflies do not make cocoons.

---

3 ## What is the life cycle of a grasshopper? ☆

Science facts
A grasshopper is an example of an insect that has the same body shape throughout most of its life.

Science quiz
Use the words to label each stage in the life of a grasshopper and complete the sentences below.

| Adult | Nymph | Egg |

Egg   Nymph

Adult

1 A grasshopper starts as a tiny __egg__, usually attached to a leaf or stem.

2 A baby grasshopper is called a __nymph__.

3 A fully grown __adult__ grasshopper has large legs for hopping.

A grasshopper's body is shaped by a strong external skeleton called an exoskeleton. As the insect grows, it sheds its old exoskeleton and a new one forms. This is called moulting and it happens many times over the life of the insect.

---

4 ☆ ## What is the life cycle of a frog?

Science facts
A frog is an amphibian, which is a type of animal that spends part of its life in water and part on land. Frogs are very different at each stage of their life cycle. The change in body shape from tadpole to adult is called metamorphosis.

Science quiz
Use the words to label the stages in the life of a frog.

| Egg | Frog | Froglet | Tadpole | Tadpole with legs |

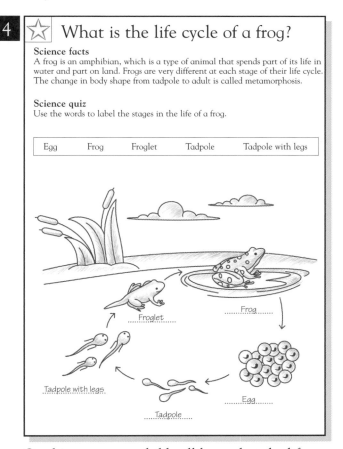

Froglet   Frog

Tadpole with legs   Egg

Tadpole

On this page, your child will learn that the life cycle of a frog is similar to that of a butterfly's. Their bodies undergo a change at each stage of the life cycle. The grasshopper, however, looks much the same throughout its life.

Why do plants have flowers?

Science facts
Flowers contain the male and female sexual organs of a plant. The petals are brightly coloured and scented to attract insects and other pollinators. The stamen (containing the anther and filament) is the male part. It produces pollen. The carpel, containing the ovary, style and stigma, is the female part. Seeds form when the male cell meets the female cell in the ovary.

Science quiz
Write the correct numbers in the circles below to show the name of each part of the flower. You may need to look in a reference book for help.

| 1 Ovary | 2 Style | 3 Anther | 4 Filament | 5 Petal | 6 Sepal | 7 Stigma |

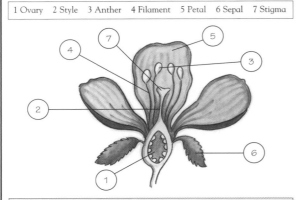

Science activity

Not all flowers have the same structure as the one shown above, but you can find all these parts in most flowers. Gather some flowers from a garden or buy some from a shop. Take them apart carefully. Display the parts of each flower by sticking the bits on a piece of white card. Label the parts.

Your child will learn the names of the reproductive parts of a flower. Choose non-poisonous flowers to dissect. Avoid using composite flowers, such as daisies or sunflowers, as the central disc in each floret is too small to dissect.

How are flowers pollinated?

Science facts
The process by which pollen gets transferred from one flower to another is called pollination. This transfer can happen in different ways. Insects such as bees are attracted to bright, scented flowers. They go into the flower to gather nectar and the spiky pollen sticks to their bodies. The sticky stigmas on other flowers catch the pollen when the insect brushes past them. Some flowers use the wind to carry pollen. Their dangling stamens produce lots of light pollen that is blown about by the wind.
The stigmas of these plants are feathery and hang outside the flower to catch the pollen as it floats by.

Science quiz
The parts of some flowers are described below. Write **Insect** if you think they belong to insect-pollinated flowers or **Wind** for wind-pollinated flowers.

1 The stigmas are sticky. .... Insect /Wind

2 The stamens are dangling out of the flower. .... Wind

3 The petals are bright red and smell nice. .... Insect

4 The stamens are inside the flower. .... Insect

5 The stigmas are feathery. .... Wind

6 The petals are small and green. .... Wind

7 The flower is very small. .... Wind

Science activity

(!) You may be surprised to know that grass has flowers. They are not very pretty or scented as they are pollinated by the wind and do not have to attract insects. In summer, try and find some grass flowers. Use a magnifying glass to look for the feathery stigmas and stamens.

Encourage your child to look for grass flowers. Explain that airborne pollen can cause hay fever. Trees such as willow, oak and ash also have flowers that are pollinated by the wind. Note that even wind-pollinated flowers have slightly sticky stigmas.

How do seeds germinate in the wild?

Science facts
Seeds need air, moisture and warmth to germinate, or sprout. They do not need soil. Some kinds of seed need to be frozen before they can germinate and a few rare species can only germinate after forest fires. Most seeds will germinate in either a light or a dark place, but some germinate faster in the dark and others in the light.

Science quiz
Explain how you could set up a fair test to show that a broad-bean seed does not need to be in the dark to germinate. Describe how you would use broad-bean seeds, cotton wool, water and two containers to set up your test.

Take two broad-bean seeds. Place a seed on some cotton wool in each container.

Soak them both well. Place one container in the light and the other in the

dark. For the test to be fair, they should both receive the same amount of

water and warmth.

Science activity

Do seeds from different plants take different amounts of time to germinate? Set up an experiment to find out. You can try germinating a variety of seeds on damp cotton wool.

Seeds take different amounts of time to germinate. For the activity, your child could try growing chick-peas, broad beans, mung beans, mustard and cress. Ask him or her to predict how long the seeds will take to germinate.

How quickly do we grow?

Science facts
Most animals have similar patterns of growth. In general, they grow when they are young and stop at adulthood. Girls and boys grow at different rates. Rates of growth and size at maturity are also affected by such things as diet and heredity. For example, tall parents are likely to have offspring who grow into tall adults.

Science quiz
These charts show the heights of some girls and boys. They were measured in Year 1, then again in Year 3 and in Year 5. Find out how much each child has grown by working out the difference between their heights in the four years between Year 1 and Year 5. Fill in each growth box.

Girls	Height in cm			
Name	Year 1	Year 3	Year 5	Growth
Susan	110	116	128	18
Dela	109	116	130	21
Farida	102	110	121	19
Jasmine	112	118	126	14

Boys	Height in cm			
Name	Year 1	Year 3	Year 5	Growth
Jack	110	115	126	16
Liang	112	119	126	14
Dave	112	120	131	19
Naresh	100	105	111	11

Which child grew the most in four years? ...... Dela grew the most.

What was the average growth of the girls? .... 18 cm

What was the average growth of the boys? .... 15 cm

Did all the girls grow at the same rate? .... No

Did all the boys grow at the same rate? .... No

Did the girls or the boys grow faster? ...... The girls grew faster.

Science activity

(!) Soak a broad-bean seed in water overnight. Plant the seed in some potting compost. Cover it with a plastic bag and leave it in a warm place, watering it regularly. After a few days, a shoot should grow. Record the shoot's height each day for two weeks. Draw a graph of the shoot's growth.

All living things grow but not necessarily at the same rate. In the *Science activity*, ensure your child measures the bean shoot accurately. The ruler should be placed gently on the soil's surface and not pushed into it.

How long is a life cycle?

Science facts
Animals and plants have life cycles. There is a period of development before they are born. This is called the gestation period. Then, there is a period of growth that leads to maturity, when they can reproduce. The offspring then begin their own life cycles. In humans, the gestation period and the time taken to reach maturity are very long. The growth phase is divided into several stages: babyhood, childhood and adolescence.

Science quiz
Study this chart carefully and answer the questions that follow.

Animal	Gestation period (days)	Age at maturity
Human	270 days	14 years
Bear	230 days	4 years
Horse	336 days	2 years
Dog	63 days	15 months
Cat	60 days	9 months
Elephant	624 days	14 years
Mouse	20 days	6 weeks

Which animal has the longest gestation period? ....Elephant...........

Which animal reaches maturity in the shortest time? ....Mouse...........

Is there a link between the age at maturity and the size of the animal?

Generally, the bigger the animal, the longer the time taken to reach maturity.

....

> ### Science activity
> Ask an adult you know well if you can have some photos of him or her as a baby, a child, an adolescent and a parent. Put the photos in order of age. Draw a time line on a big piece of paper. Mark each year on it and stick the photos beside the right years. Label each stage of development.

Living things must reproduce or become extinct. Your child should understand that the life cycle ensures the continuation of a species. For the activity, encourage your child to guess the time span between photographs before being told.

Which metal is this?

Science facts
A metal is a type of material. Almost all metals are shiny, malleable (can be hammered into different shapes) and conduct heat and electricity. There are different types of metal, such as iron, copper, gold, lead and tin. Each metal has a set of additional properties that makes it unique.

Science quiz
Use the branching Yes/No key below to identify each of the five metals in this chart. Write the correct letter for each metal below its name.

	Properties
A	Hard; brown in colour; good conductor of electricity
B	Relatively soft; yellow colour; does not tarnish; very good conductor of electricity
C	Soft; silver colour; tarnishes quickly; very heavy; a weak conductor of electricity
D	Hard; silver colour; magnetic; tarnishes easily (rusts)
E	Hard; silver colour; does not tarnish easily; not magnetic

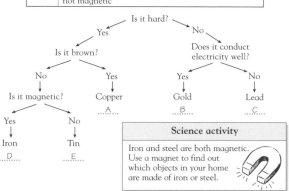

Is it hard?
- Yes → Is it brown?
  - No → Is it magnetic?
    - Yes → Iron ...D...
    - No → Tin ...E...
  - Yes → Copper ...A...
- No → Does it conduct electricity well?
  - Yes → Gold ...B...
  - No → Lead ...C...

> ### Science activity
> Iron and steel are both magnetic. Use a magnet to find out which objects in your home are made of iron or steel.

Your child can use a magnet to check the magnetic properties of objects such as pipes, cutlery, toys, appliances, coins and keys. Note that some stainless steel cutlery may not be magnetic, while some coins made of copper-coated steel are magnetic.

Is it an electrical conductor?

Science facts
A material that allows electricity to pass through it easily is called an electrical conductor. Many metals are good electrical conductors.

Science quiz
An electrical circuit was set up to test whether or not some materials are conductors. If the material conducts electricity, the bulb in the circuit lights up. The better the conductor, the brighter the bulb. Here are the results.

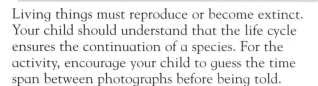

Material tested	Status of lamp
Gold	Very bright
Copper	Bright
Plastic	Not lit
Wood	Not lit
Graphite	Quite bright
Lead	Quite bright
Paper	Not lit
Sea water	Bright
Pure water	Not lit

Most metals conduct electricity. Can you identify the metals in the chart?
Gold, copper and lead.

Which one is the best conductor? *Gold is the best conductor.*

Which solid non-metal conducts electricity? Where do you usually find this?
Graphite conducts electricity. It is often found in pencils.

Why do you think sea water conducts electricity but pure water does not?
The dissolved salt in sea water makes it conduct electricity.

> ### Science activity
> (!) Make a circuit using a battery, wires and a bulb. Use your circuit to find some more materials that conduct electricity.

Assist your child in testing the conductivity of different materials. Metals are generally good conductors of electricity. Two non-metallic conductors are: graphite, a form of carbon found in pencil "lead" and sea water, which contains salt.

Is it a thermal insulator?

Science facts
Materials that allow heat to pass through them easily are called thermal conductors. Metals and glass are good thermal conductors. Some materials do not conduct heat well. They are called thermal insulators. Materials such as plastics, wood, wool and air are good thermal insulators.

Science quiz
Five glasses containing water at 60°C were each wrapped in a different material. After 10 minutes, the water temperature in each glass was recorded. The results are shown in the table below.

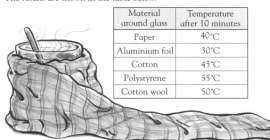

Material around glass	Temperature after 10 minutes
Paper	40°C
Aluminium foil	30°C
Cotton	45°C
Polystyrene	55°C
Cotton wool	50°C

Which material would you choose to wrap around a water pipe in winter to stop the water from freezing? Explain why.

I would wrap polystyrene around a water pipe to stop the water from freezing because the experiment shows that it is the best thermal insulator – it kept the water warm the longest.

> ### Science activity
> Fill two yogurt pots with water. Record the temperature in each pot and then put on the lids. Cover one pot in a thick layer of lard. Put them both in a freezer for 20 minutes and then record the water temperature again. What do your results tell you about why whales and seals living in cold waters have thick layers of body fat?

The quiz shows that some materials are better thermal insulators than others. For the activity, encourage your child to predict which yogurt pot will stay warmer and why. He or she will learn that body fat is a good thermal insulator.

How soluble are materials?

Science facts
Substances that can be dissolved in a liquid are said to be soluble. Those that do not dissolve are said to be insoluble. The liquid in which a substance dissolves is called a solvent. The substance that is dissolved is called a solute. Together, they make a solution. Water is a good solvent: it dissolves many substances but not all. Sugar and salt both dissolve in water, while substances such as chalk and sand are insoluble.

Science quiz
Shakira collected two different plant fertilisers from a garden centre. She was told to mix each fertiliser with water and then to sprinkle the solution on her plants. When she mixed them, the first substance "disappeared". The fertiliser in the second can sank to the bottom.

The fertiliser in the second watering can would not be very effective. Why?
It would not be effective because it is insoluble. It would not mix with
the water and so would not be taken up by the plants' roots.

Science activity
Collect some substances such as flour, Epsom salts, icing sugar, sand, baking powder, bicarbonate of soda and cooking oil. Design a way of finding out which substances are soluble in water and which are insoluble.

Ask your child how he or she will know if a substance has dissolved. What will your child look for? Make sure that your child uses only small quantities of the solutes (baking powder, etc.) so that it is easy to see whether or not they dissolve.

Are all substances equally soluble?

Science facts
All soluble substances do not dissolve equally well. Sugar dissolves very easily, while other substances, such as salt, dissolve less easily. The amount of solute that will dissolve in a solvent is a measure of its solubility.

Science quiz
Below is a graph showing the solubility of different substances.

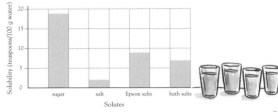

About how many spoonfuls of salt dissolve in the water? ......2......

About how many spoonfuls of bath salts dissolve in the water? ......7......

Another substance is more soluble than bath salts but less soluble than Epsom salts. What range of spoonfuls would you expect to dissolve? ....7–9....

List the solutes in the chart in order of their solubility. Write the name of the most soluble substance first.

........Sugar........ ....Epsom salts.... ....Bath salts.... ....Salt........

Science activity
Does the grain size of sugar affect its solubility? Design and carry out an experiment to answer this question.

Ask your child to predict which size of sugar grain will dissolve more quickly in water and why. Help him or her plan an experiment. To make it fair, encourage your child to use the same amount of sugar and water in each instance.

Can you separate salt from sand?

Science facts
Filtering removes insoluble particles from water (particles that do not dissolve). Salt is soluble in water, but sand is not soluble (it is insoluble). The water in a salt solution will evaporate if it is left uncovered. Rock salt is a mixture of salt and sand.

Science quiz
Using the information above, explain how you could separate the salt from a piece of rock salt. Drawing a flowchart might help.

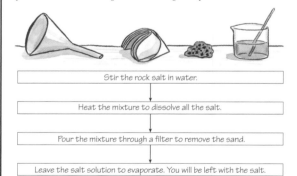

Stir the rock salt in water.

Heat the mixture to dissolve all the salt.

Pour the mixture through a filter to remove the sand.

Leave the salt solution to evaporate. You will be left with the salt.

Science activity
What type of paper makes the best filter? Design an experiment to find out. You will need a funnel and different kinds of paper, including newspaper, writing paper, blotting paper, wrapping paper and tissue paper.

Help your child design the experiment for the activity. Ask questions such as, "What shall we filter?", "What should we look at to find out which paper filters best?", "How about looking at how clear the water is after filtration?"

Can we filter things?

Science facts
If the materials in a mixture are insoluble, you can use a filter to separate them. A filter has holes in it. Coffee grounds are insoluble in water. When you pour a mixture of coffee grounds and water into a filter, the holes in the filter are large enough for the liquid to drain away, but too small for the grounds to pass through. The coffee grounds are trapped by the filter.

Science quiz
Here are some lentils, peas and marbles all mixed up in a pot. Pictures A and B show the bottom of the pot. On A, draw the sizes of holes you must make to separate the lentils from the peas and marbles. On B, draw the holes you would need to make to separate the lentils and peas from the marbles.

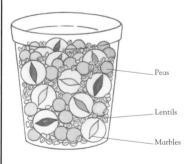

Peas

Lentils

Marbles

Science activity
(!) Try filtering out the different sized particles of soil. You can use a flowerpot with holes in it to remove larger stones. Then squeeze the remains through an old pair of tights. Only the tiniest soil particles will get through. (Always wear gloves when you handle soil.)

Your child will learn that some mixtures can be separated by filtration. In every filter, the size of the holes determines the size of the particles it will allow through. Help your child use coffee filters, colanders and sieves to separate different mixtures.

How can we separate mixtures?

Science facts
Mixtures of materials can be separated in different ways. To find out which is the best way to separate a mixture, you must first ask yourself some important questions. For example, are any of the materials in the mixture soluble? Are any of the materials attracted to a magnet? Do any of the materials change when they are heated? What size are the particles in the materials?

Science quiz
On the left, you can see four different mixtures. On the right are four different methods of separating mixtures. Draw a line between each mixture and the correct separation method.

Steel nails and copper nails

Rice and mung beans

Soil containing mud and sand

Sand and salt

Dissolve in water and then use a filter.

Use a magnet.

Use a colander.

Shake in a bottle with some water and leave to settle.

> **Science activity**
> ⚠ Dissolve sugar in a cup of tea. Ask an adult to heat the tea in a saucepan until almost all the water has boiled away. If you leave the remains to dry out for a few days, what happens?

Your child will learn that the method used to separate a mixture depends on the properties of the materials it contains. This will require advanced thinking. Encourage your child to justify his or her answers by saying: "These will separate because…"

☆

Which fabric will stretch the most?

Science facts
Materials that stretch easily are called elastic materials. Some materials are more elastic than others. We can compare the elasticity of two materials by hanging equal weights from them and measuring how much they stretch.

Science quiz
Poppy tried to compare the stretch in five different fabrics. All the fabrics were the same length to begin with. Her table of results is shown below.

Fabric	Weight hung from fabric	Amount of stretch
Cotton	10 N	3 cm
Wool	100 N	40 cm
Nylon	100 N	55 cm
Polyester	500 N	200 cm
Tercel	10 N	3 cm

Which material stretched the most?
Nylon stretched the most. It stretched 5.5 cm for every 10 N.

How could Poppy have improved her experiment?
Poppy could have improved her experiment by using the same weight
each time to allow a comparison to be made more easily.

> **Science activity**
> Design an experiment to find out which brand of tights stretches the most.

From the table in the quiz, it may seem that polyester stretched the most, but that is because Poppy used a greater weight to stretch it. For the activity, encourage your child to design a fair test, using the same weight for each brand of tights.

Which is the strongest wood? ☆

Science facts
Strength is an important property of materials. It is a measure of a material's resistance to breaking. You can compare the strengths of different materials by hanging increasingly heavier weights from them until they break.

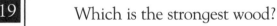

500 N

Science quiz
Lata hung weights on strips of wood until the wood broke in the middle.

Type of wood	Weight needed to break wood (in newtons)
Beech	2000 N
Oak	3000 N
Walnut	2600 N
Ash	2500 N
Pine	500 N
Sycamore	2500 N

Use the data in the table above to work out which type of wood you would choose to build a bridge. Explain your choice.
I would choose oak to build a bridge because the experiment shows
that it is the strongest wood.

> **Science activity**
> ⚠ Collect some twigs of the same width from different types of tree. Hang a bag from each twig and then suspend the twigs between two table tops. Load each bag with the same weight (such as a can of beans) until the twigs break. Which is the strongest twig?

Your child will learn how to compare the strength of different materials. Oak was the strongest of the woods tested, but was it a fair test? The experiment would only be fair if all the twigs were of the same length and thickness.

☆

Are some changes reversible?

Science facts
When ice is warmed, it melts to form water. When water is heated further, it evaporates or boils to form water vapour. These changes from solid to liquid to gas can be reversed by cooling water vapour. The water vapour will condense to form water, and the water will freeze to form ice.

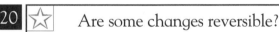

Ice	melts → ← freezes	Water	boils → ← condenses	Water vapour

Science quiz
Explain what is happening to the water in each picture.
The water vapour is condensing to form water droplets
on the cold window pane.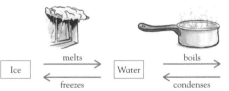

 _The water in the wet washing is evaporating_
to form water vapour.

The water vapour in the air is changing to water and
then quickly to ice on a very cold day.

> **Science activity**
> Light a candle and watch it carefully (do not touch it or get too close). Can you identify the solid wax, melted wax and wax vapour? Can you see the liquid wax solidifying when the flame is put out?

Candle wax melts to form a liquid. Your child will notice that the candle flame starts a little way up the wick. This is because the heat from the flame vaporises the molten wax to form invisible wax vapour. It is the wax vapour that burns.

21 — Are some changes irreversible?

Science facts
When you mix substances together, they may change to form new substances. The changes can be reversible or irreversible. For instance, when vinegar is mixed with bicarbonate of soda, the two fizz and a new substance is formed. This change is irreversible. A change is likely to be irreversible if there is a reaction, such as a fizz or a temperature change.

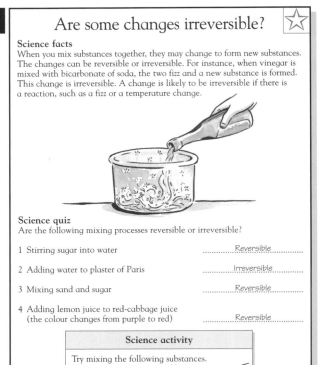

Science quiz
Are the following mixing processes reversible or irreversible?

1 Stirring sugar into water .... Reversible ....

2 Adding water to plaster of Paris .... Irreversible ....

3 Mixing sand and sugar .... Reversible ....

4 Adding lemon juice to red-cabbage juice
(the colour changes from purple to red) .... Reversible ....

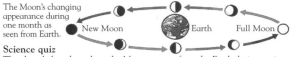

Science activity
Try mixing the following substances.
Which changes are reversible?
1 Lemon juice added to baking powder
2 Vinegar added to chalk
3 Vinegar added to salt
4 Lemon juice added to sugar

Adding an alkali will reverse the colour change in the fourth question in the quiz. Lemon juice and vinegar are acids. They will fizz and produce carbon dioxide when added to carbonates, such as chalk and baking powder.

22 — Where is each planet?

Science facts
There are eight planets in the solar system. In order from the Sun, they are: Mercury, Venus, Earth, Mars, Jupiter, Saturn, Uranus and Neptune.

Science quiz
The planets are shown here in their order from the Sun. Label each one correctly. They are not shown to scale.

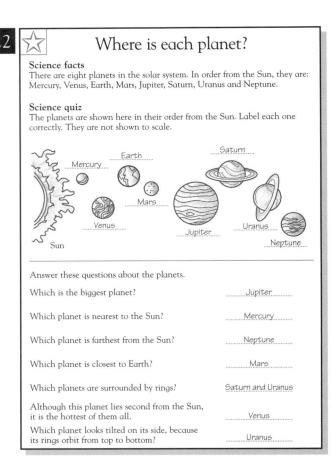

Answer these questions about the planets.

Which is the biggest planet? .... Jupiter

Which planet is nearest to the Sun? .... Mercury

Which planet is farthest from the Sun? .... Neptune

Which planet is closest to Earth? .... Mars

Which planets are surrounded by rings? .... Saturn and Uranus

Although this planet lies second from the Sun, it is the hottest of them all. .... Venus

Which planet looks tilted on its side, because its rings orbit from top to bottom? .... Uranus

Mercury, Venus, Mars, Jupiter and Saturn are visible to the naked eye from Earth. Of these, Venus is the easiest to spot. With your child, research online the current position of these planets above your area and see if you can spot them.

23 — Does the Moon change shape?

Science facts
The Moon is not a light source. Light from the Sun is reflected off the surface of the Moon, allowing us to see it. The Moon makes a complete orbit around the Earth in about 28 days. You can see either a whole, round Moon reflecting light or just a part of it depending on where it is in its orbit.

The Moon's changing appearance during one month as seen from Earth.

New Moon — Earth — Full Moon

Science quiz
The chart below shows how the Moon appears from the Earth during various dates in January. Can you work out the missing shapes?

Date in January	Moon's appearance
1st	🌑
6th	🌘
10th	🌗
15th	🌕
19th	🌓
24th	🌒
28th	🌑

Science activity
You can model the way the Moon appears as it orbits the Earth. Use a torch to represent the Sun and a table-tennis ball for the Moon. Ask a friend to hold the torch still in a darkened room. Hold the ball at arm's length in front of the torch. Turn around slowly in a circle, keeping your eyes fixed on the ball. Can you see the reflection of the light on the ball? Does it look like the different phases of the Moon?

Here, your child will learn why the Moon appears to change shape. For the activity, you will need a good torch and a darkened room to see the changing reflections of the light on the ball. Encourage your child to watch the ball carefully.

24 — What shape is the Earth?

Science facts
Stars and planets are spherical. Stars are balls of burning gas that produce heat and light. Planets are made of rock, gas and sometimes frozen liquid. Some have spherical moons that travel around them. Our Solar System contains a star, called the Sun, and eight planets.

Science quiz
Imagine you are travelling in a spacecraft and are able to look out of the window at our part of the Solar System. Which of these pictures would you be most likely to see? Tick (✔) the right box.

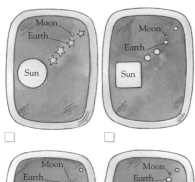

Science activity
Find out the names of the eight planets in the Solar System. What is each planet made of? Which is the biggest planet and which is the smallest? Which of the planets have moons? Use books or the Internet to find out the answers.

Your child needs to know that the Sun, Earth and Moon are roughly spherical. Children find it interesting to know the composition and size of other planets and to compare them with the Earth.

25 Why does the Sun appear to move? ☆

Science facts
The Sun appears to move across the sky during the course of the day. In fact, it is the Earth that moves and not the Sun. The Earth makes one complete turn around its axis every 24 hours, or once a day. The Sun appears to rise in the east, when the part of the Earth you are on is turning towards the Sun, and appears to set in the west, when your hometown is turning away from the Sun. As well as spinning on its axis, the Earth orbits around the Sun. It takes the Earth 365 days, or one year, to make one complete orbit around the Sun.

Science quiz
The picture shows the Sun at three times during one day. First it was in position A, then B and finally C.

Which side of the picture is the east? _____ The left side is east. _____

What time is it at position B? _____ Midday – 12 o'clock _____

About what time is it at position C? _____ About 4 o'clock in the afternoon _____

Science activity
On a sunny morning, stand a 50-cm-long stick in the ground in your garden or local park. Mark the position of the end of the stick's shadow with a piece of chalk. Repeat this every hour so that by evening you have at least seven marks on the ground. What pattern can you see? Explain why the shadow moved.

The apparent movement of the Sun is caused by the Earth's rotation on its axis. For the activity, your child should notice that the shadow gets shorter as midday approaches. It then appears to move to the other side and becomes longer again.

26 ☆ What causes night and day?

Science facts
The Earth completes one turn around its axis every 24 hours. When the part of the Earth where you live faces the Sun, it is daytime. Sunrise, also called dawn, occurs when the part of the Earth where you are turns enough for you to just see the Sun. At sunset, just before night, the Earth has turned so that again you can only just see the Sun. When it is night where you are, it is daytime for people living on the other side of the Earth.

Science quiz
One evening, David, who lives in London, England, was allowed to phone his uncle who lives in Montreal, Canada. David was very surprised to hear that his uncle was just about to have his midday meal.

What is the explanation for this difference in time?

Canada is west of England. Sunrise in Montreal occurs about 5 hours after sunrise in England. The clocks there are set at a different time. When it is 5 o'clock in England, it is midday in Montreal.

Science activity
Make a model of the Sun and the Earth. Use a torch to represent the Sun and a football to represent the Earth. Do this experiment in a darkened room. Put your torch on a table so that it shines into the room. Hold the football about 1 metre away from the torch and turn it around slowly. The football is like the Earth turning on its axis. Draw a mark on your ball with a pencil. Spin your ball slowly. Notice how the light only falls on the mark for about half of the spin. This is like daytime. When the light does not shine on the mark, it is like night.

For the activity, ask your child to tell you what is happening at the marked place on the model of the Earth. Help him or her identify when it would be sunrise or sunset at that spot.

27 What makes things fall? ☆

Science facts
Gravity is a type of force. It is a pull, or force of attraction, between two objects. The bigger the object, the bigger the attraction. The Earth is a huge object and everything on the Earth is pulled towards the Earth's centre. We call the pull between us and the Earth our weight. Force is measured in units called newtons. The pull of gravity on us, our weight, can be measured in newtons. The force on each kilogram is about 10 newtons. This means that the heavier you are, the more force gravity has on you.

Science quiz
Draw an arrow to show the direction of the force extending the spring.

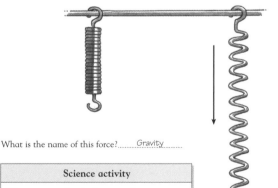

What is the name of this force? _____ Gravity _____

Science activity
When you stand on bathroom scales, you can find out how heavy you are in kilograms (kg). Use your bathroom scales to work out how much force you exert on the Earth due to gravity pulling you down. Remember, the force on 1 kilogram is 10 newtons.

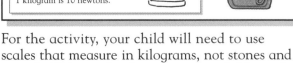

For the activity, your child will need to use scales that measure in kilograms, not stones and pounds. If the scales show that your child weighs 30 kg (about 5 stones), he or she exerts a force of 300 N on the Earth (i.e. 10 x 30 kg).

28 ☆ Does a force have a direction?

Science facts
A force is a push or a pull. Forces can move things or stop them from moving. They can make things speed up or slow down. Forces can also make things change direction. For example, the force of the wind can blow a boat off course. A force acts in one direction. This direction is shown in diagrams by using arrows. A longer arrow is used to show a bigger force.

A gentle kick   A hard kick

Science quiz
Look at the diagrams below. On each diagram, draw an arrow to show the direction of each force mentioned.

The pull of gravity on the spring	The force of friction slowing the rolling can

The force of the hammer	The force exerted by each team (2 arrows)

Science activity
Use a newtonmeter to measure some forces. Compare the forces needed to open a door, to drag a pencil case or to lift a cup. Then, draw each object and use an arrow to show the direction in which the newtonmeter is pulled.

Forces make things speed up, slow down, start, stop or change direction. Encourage your child to estimate the force needed to do various tasks such as lifting a spoon and then check the estimates with the newtonmeter.

How do parachutes work?

Science facts

Gravity is a pulling force. It pulls objects towards the Earth. Air resistance is a pushing force. Parachutes use air resistance to slow down falling objects. The air caught under the parachute pushes against the fabric's surface, slowing it down. The bigger the parachute, the more slowly it will fall. This is because more air pushes against larger surfaces and so there is more air resistance.

Air resistance

Gravity

Science quiz

Look at this drawing of two people jumping with parachutes.

Which one will fall to Earth faster? Explain your answer.

The small parachute will fall faster to Earth because it provides less surface

area for air to act on. There is less air resistance.

What is the name of the force pulling the people and their parachutes down?

Gravity

Science activity

Find out if your answers in the quiz are correct. Make two parachutes using handkerchiefs or paper towels, cotton thread and two identical small weights, such as nuts. Make one parachute larger than the other. Drop them from the same height. Which one falls faster?

To make the comparison fair, the nuts on the parachutes should be the same weight. Try to make the parachutes quite different in size. A small hole cut in the centre of each one will help the chutes drop in a straight line.

What makes boats float?

Science facts

An object floats or sinks depending on a combination of the object's shape and weight. When an object is placed in water, the water pushes the object upwards – this force is called the upthrust. If enough water pushes it up, the upthrust will be greater than gravity and the object will float.

Upthrust   Gravity

Science quiz

Objects weigh less in water than in air because of the upthrust of water. David used a newtonmeter to measure and compare the weights of different objects in air and in water. His results are given in the table below.

Object	Weight in air (N)	Weight in water (N)
Stone	130 N	6 N
Wood block	20 N	0 N
Plastic hair clip	5 N	1 N
Metal pan	500 N	0 N

Use the table above to work out which objects will float. Explain how you came to your conclusions.

The wood block and metal pan will float because they weigh nothing in water.

Science activity

Take a lump of modelling clay. Place it in a bowl of water. Does it float or sink? Can you find a way to shape the clay so that it will float? How many shapes can you make that will float? Can you explain why these shapes float?

In answering the quiz, encourage your child to use the information in the table rather than making a guess. The broad, flat shape of the metal pan also helps it float because more water pushes up against a larger surface area.

What effect does friction have?

Science facts

Friction is a force that slows things down. Whenever two surfaces come into contact, there is a frictional force. The amount of frictional force (how much it slows things down) depends on the roughness of the surfaces and on the force pressing them together. For example, if two plastic balls of the same size but different weights are given a push of the same strength, the lighter ball will go farther because there is less friction slowing it down.

Science quiz

Amber covered a plank with different materials and measured how far a wooden block slid on each surface before coming to a halt. Here are her results.

Type of surface	How far the block slid after being pushed
Sandpaper	50 cm
Glass	500 cm
Wood	100 cm
Plastic	300 cm
Cardboard	190 cm

Which is the smoothest surface and which is the roughest surface?

Glass is the smoothest surface and sandpaper is the roughest.

Explain how you worked out the answers to the question above.

Rough surfaces slow things down because there is more friction. The block slid

farthest on glass so it must be the smoothest surface.

Science activity

Use a plank of wood, a toy block, sticky tape, and different materials, such as paper, polythene and sandpaper, to compare the roughness of their surfaces. Tape one material to the plank. Place the block on it and lift one end of the plank until the block slides down. Repeat with the other materials. Which material provides the most friction?

Friction is a force that slows things down – the rougher the surface, the greater the friction. How high the plank has to be lifted is a measure of the roughness of the surface tested in the activity. The block will slide farther on smoother surfaces.

How does a lever work?

Science facts

The point at which a lever turns is called a fulcrum. The fulcrum needs to be in the right place for the lever to work properly.

Science quiz

Using the objects pictured below, carry out the instructions.

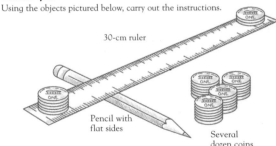

30-cm ruler

Pencil with flat sides

Several dozen coins

1 Set up the test as shown above. The ruler is the lever.
2 Slide the pencil under the ruler at the 10-cm mark. This is the lever's fulcrum, or pivot.
3 Stack 5 coins between the end of the ruler and the 2.5-cm mark.
4 At the other end of the ruler, stack coins one at a time until the end with the 5 coins rises off the table.
5 Place the pencil at different positions under the ruler, as shown in the table on the right, and repeat the test.
6 Record the number of coins it takes to lift the 5 coins with the fulcrum at each of the different positions.

Answers may vary

Position of pencil under ruler	Number of coins
7.5 cm	
10 cm	
12.5 cm	
15 cm	

Levers come in many forms. Help your child identify the fulcrums and levers when: playing on a seesaw; cutting paper with a pair of scissors; using a hammer to pull a nail out of a board; using a bottle opener to remove the cap from a bottle.